I0017499

Reverse Engineering ARM Embedded Systems with STM32 Microcontrollers

A Practical Approach

By Yury Magda

To my wife, Julia

About the Author

Yury Magda is an embedded engineer experienced in designing hardware and software for Intel x86- and ARM-based systems. He is also the author of the books on designing embedded systems based upon various development platforms.

CONTENTS

Introduction

The aim of this book is to uncover practical methods for reverse engineering embedded systems based on STM32 ARM microcontrollers. The material in this book illustrates various approaches applied by the author for reversing embedded applications without any source code or binary executables. The author assumes that the readers are accustomed to creating and debugging embedded system software and hardware. While analyzing and debugging embedded systems, the STM32CubeProgrammer, Keil uVision IDE and Debugger, IAR Embedded Workbench for ARM and GHIDRA Disassembler were used.

Disclaimer

While the author has used good faith efforts to ensure that the information and instructions contained in this book are accurate, the author disclaims all responsibility for errors or omissions, including without limitation responsibility for damages resulting from the use of or reliance on this work. Use of the information and instructions contained in this work is at your own risk. If any code samples or other technology this book contains or describes is subject to open source licenses or the intellectual property rights of others, it is your responsibility to ensure that your use thereof complies with such licenses and/or rights. All example applications from this book were developed and tested without damaging hardware. The author will not accept any responsibility for damages of any kind due to actions taken by you after reading this book.

The basic concepts

Performing reverse engineering on an embedded system requires a combination of hardware and software skills. If we know the type of microcontroller used in the externally produced embedded system board, investigating it becomes much easier. Below are listed steps that you can take to analyze such a board:

1. **Obtaining the documentation on a microcontroller**. Usually, we need the datasheet and reference manual. These documents give us

the necessary information about the microcontroller's pinout, timing, and other important parameters.

2. **Identifying the Input and Output Pins**: Based on the datasheet, identify the input and output pins of the microcontroller. Use a logic analyzer or an oscilloscope to observe the signals on these pins and try to identify their patterns.

3. **Developing a Hypothesis**: Based on the observed input and output signals, develop a hypothesis about the board's functionality. Try to understand how the inputs are processed to generate the outputs. It may be helpful to use a block diagram to visualize the different components of the system.

4. **Experimenting with the Inputs**: Experiment with different input signals to try understand how the board responds. You can use a function generator or a signal generator to generate different input signals and observe the outputs.

5. **Experimenting with outputs using a logic analyzer and / or oscilloscope:** The logic analyzer / oscilloscope can be used to monitor the signals between the microcontroller and other components, such as sensors or actuators. By examining the signals on the microcontroller pins, it may be possible to determine how the microcontroller is processing data and communicating with other devices.

6. **Obtaining the embedded code**. If the system provides debugging features, such as a JTAG/SWD interface, it may be possible to connect to the system and analyze its behavior using a debugger. This can help identify how the system is functioning and potentially identify any issues.

7. **Reverse engineering the embedded code**: Reverse engineering involves analyzing the behavior of a system to understand how it works without access to the original design or source code. This can be done by examining the hardware, firmware, and software of the system. Tools such as disassemblers and decompilers can be used to reverse engineer the code and understand its functionality. It is important to note that modifying firmware can be a complex process, and there is a risk of introducing errors or unintended behavior into the system. You should have a thorough understanding of the firmware and the hardware before attempting to modify it, and be prepared to spend time testing and debugging your modifications.

8. **Downloading** the patched code to the flash memory of a microcontroller using the JTAG/SWD interface.
9. **Debugging**: If the system provides debugging features, such as a JTAG/SWD interface, it may be possible to connect to the system and analyze its behavior using a debugger. This can help identify how the system is functioning and potentially identify any issues.
10. **Testing**: Testing the system in various scenarios can help to identify its behavior and functionality. For example, sending different inputs to the system and observing its outputs can help to identify how it processes data and what its expected behavior is.

Overall, analyzing embedded systems without access to the source code can be a challenging task, but with the right tools and techniques, it is possible to gain a better understanding of how the system works and identify any potential issues.

Being accustomed to the embedded systems with STM32 microcontrollers, I adapted the above sequence to use with these microcontrollers.

Since I work with the STM32 application boards, I use the following sequence:
1. Identify the microcontroller (MCU) architecture and the instruction set of the ARM processor. This is the most important step - we can't continue if we don't know what MCU is used in some particular board;
2. If the first step was successful, I determine how the ARM board is powered and what external circuits (if any) are connected to the board. Often the application board comes without any external hardware that makes further investigation more complex;
3. Connect a debug probe (I use the ST-LINK debug probe) to the SWD interface of a microcontroller;
4. Launch the STM32CubeProgrammer tool and read the flash memory of an MCU;
5. Estimate the size of the code read from flash;
6. Save the code in a HEX-file;
7. Try to reverse engineering the saved HEX-file using the GHIDRA Disassembler / Decompiler;
8. If reverse engineering shows too complex disassembly and / or may take long time, I use the Keil uVision IDE tool to debug the STM32 microcontroller. This helps me to clarify the code in the MCU flash

and continue to reverse engineering code. Then I repeat step (7) and move to the step (9);

9. Determine the instruction(s) and / or data to be patched;
10. Patch the code;
11. Export the patched code to the new HEX-file;
12. Download the updated HEX-file (with a new name!) into the MCU flash and restart the microcontroller.

It's important to note that the above sequence is approximate and may be extended if needed. For example, sometimes I should examine the external circuitry in more detail to understand how the embedded system works. determine the full picture.

Below are the practical examples of analyzing, and modifying real STM32 embedded systems.

Example 1

In this example, we examine the application board with the STM32F401 MCU. Controlling a water pump's DC motor was one of the tasks this board carried out (**Fig.1**).

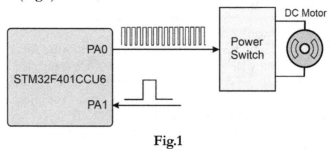

Fig.1

Initially, the PWM signal on pin **PA0** of the microcontroller controlled a DC motor for 10 s after a rising edge arrived on pin **PA1**. This is illustrated by a timing diagram in **Fig.2**.

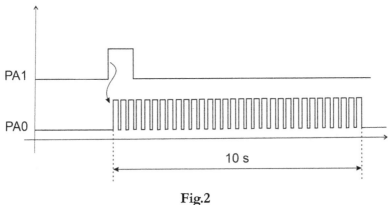

Fig.2

Later, a new, better-performing pump was installed in place of the old one. It turned out that the time interval needed for PWM to control the DC motor of the new pump needed to be reduced from 10 s to 5 s.
In this case, the timing diagram should have looked like that in **Fig.3**.

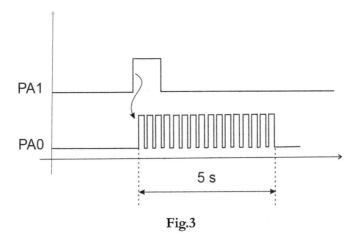

Fig.3

I thought that the problem could be solved without fully rewriting the whole embedded code but by modifying a small code block using a reverse engineering tool like the GHIDRA Disassembler/Decompiler. After investigating the application, I found out that the PWM signal was provided by Channel 1 of Timer 2.

After that I performed the following steps:

9

1. Connected the ST-LINK debug probe to the SWD interface of STM32F401;
2. Read the contents of the flash memory of the MCU using the STM32CubeProgrammer tool;
3. Determined the size of code;
4. Saved the data read by STM32CubeProgrammer in a HEX-file;
5. Reversed this HEX-file using GHIDRA (I used v 10.2.3);
6. Patched the selected code fragment and exported the memory content into a new HEX-file;
7. Downloaded the updated HEX-file into the flash memory of the MCU.;
8. Tested the embedded application.

Let's consider the above steps in detail.

Getting embedded code

After connecting the ST-Link probe to STM32F401, I launched STM32CubeProgrammer (**Fig.4**).

Fig.4

In the STM32CubeProgrammer window, it was necessary to establish the connection between the ST-Link debug probe and application board with the STM32F401 microcontroller. That was done by clicking **"Connect"** (**Fig.5**).

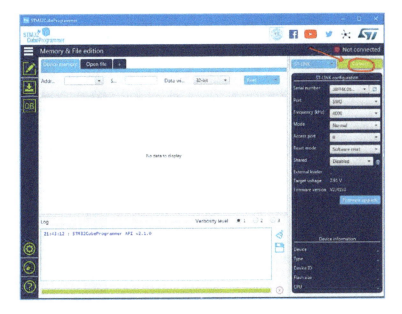

Fig.5

Once the connection had been established, the utility read the flash memory of the MCU and displayed the first 1024 bytes on the screen (**Fig.6**).

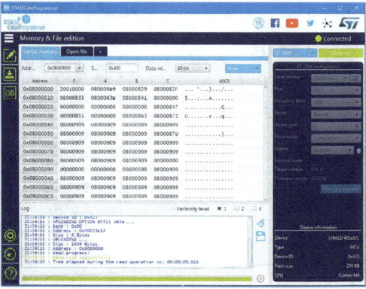

Fig.6

At the next step, it was necessary to determine the size of the binary code written in the flash memory. To do that, I changed the **"Size"** parameter a few times so that I could find out the sequence **"00FF"**. When **"00FF"** was found, it was easy to calculate the size of the binary code to be saved in the HEX-file.

In my particular case, it was necessary to write 0x2154 bytes into the HEX-file (**Fig.7**).

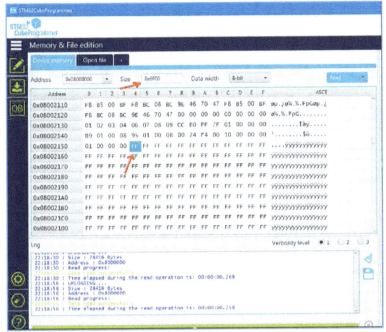

Fig.7

I set the value 0x2155 in the **"Size"** field, then clicked **"Read"** (**Fig.8**).

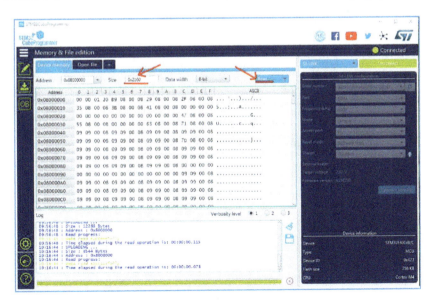

Fig.8

When I was done, I clicked **"Read"** again and chose **"Save As..."** (**Fig.9**).

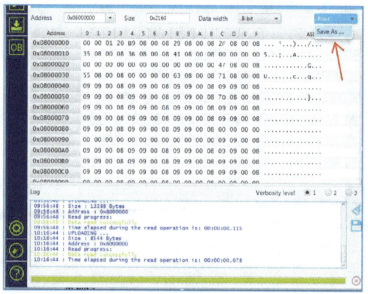

Fig.9

In the **"Save As"** dialog box, I entered the filename (**example1.hex**) and clicked **"Save"** (**Fig.10**).

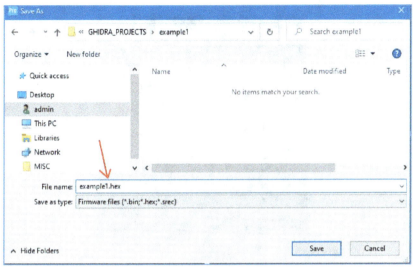

Fig.10

I saved the file in the "GHIDRA_PROJECTS\example1" directory for further processing by the GHIDRA Disassembler. I also closed the STM32CubeProgrammer.

At the next step, I analyzed **example1.hex**.

Reversing embedded code in GHIDRA

Once I had the HEX-file **example1.hex**, I reversed it using the GHIDRA Disassembler / Decompiler (**Fig.11**). GHIDRA is a popular software reverse engineering framework created by the National Security Agency (NSA). This framework includes a suite of tools for analyzing (reversing) binary code. One of the key features of GHIDRA is its Disassembler that can be used to convert machine code into assembly code.

I expected to modify **example1.hex** using GHIDRA so that I could reduce the period when the PWM output was enabled from 10 to 5 seconds.

15

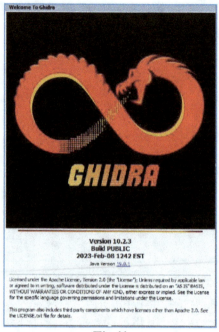

Fig.11

First, I created a new project in GHIDRA (**Fig.12**).

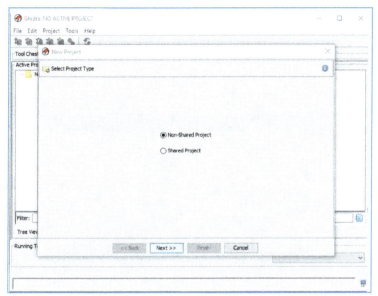

Fig.12

I imported the **example1.hex** file into the project that I named **"example1"** (**Fig.13** - **Fig.16**).

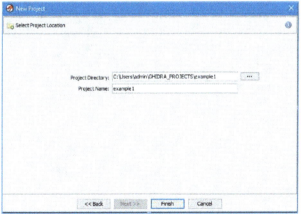

Fig.13

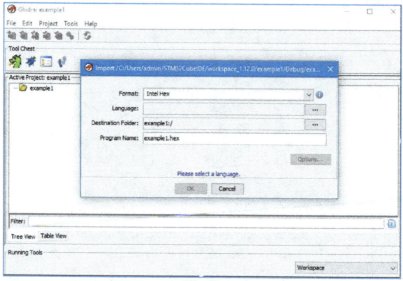

Fig.14

Then I chose the language **ARM:LE:32:v8T** (**Fig.15** - **Fig.16**).
Note that the choice of language is essential for obtaining the correct disassembly. There can be occasions when it is necessary to keep trying different languages until a suitable result is obtained.

18

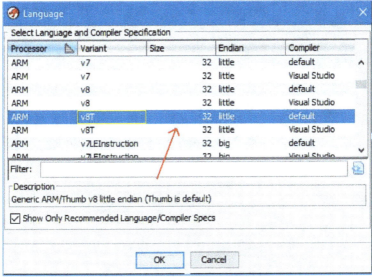

Fig.15

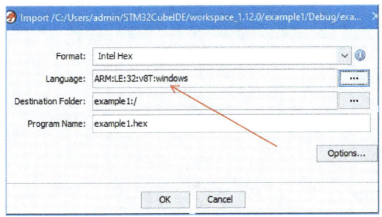

Fig.16

Next, the HEX-file parameters were displayed in the following window (**Fig. 17**).

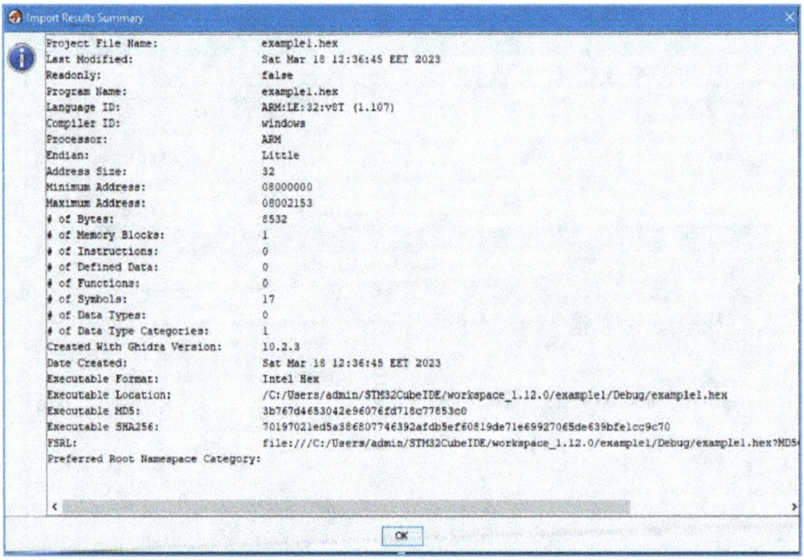

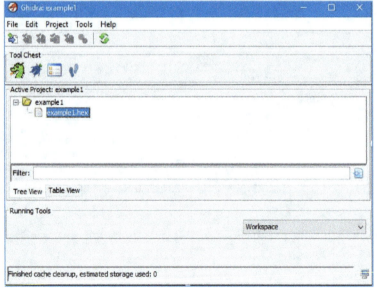

Fig.17

Finally, I got the project with the imported file **example1.hex** (**Fig.18**).

Fig.18

When **example1.hex** was dropped onto CodeBrowser, the following
window appeared (**Fig.19**).

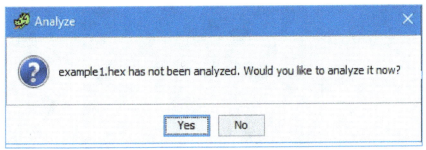

Fig.19

When in the next window (**Fig.20**) the default analysis options appeared, I
clicked "**Analyze**".

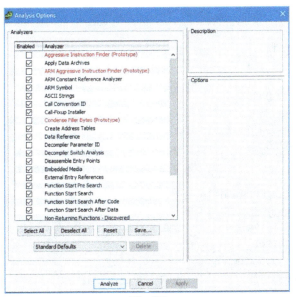

Fig.20

Once the analysis was complete, I tried to find where the **main()** function began by going through the disassembly. This gave me the function FUN_080004d8() that looked very similar to what I expected to see (**Fig.21**).

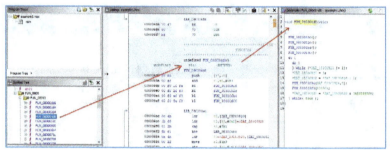

Fig.21

In order to make analysis easier, I assigned this function the name **"main"** and carefully reviewed the code inside. The information provided by GHIDRA's main() C code (**Listing 1**) was really useful to me.

Listing 1.

void main(void)

```
{
  FUN_0800090c();
  FUN_0800052c();
  FUN_080006b4();
  FUN_08000600();
  do {
    do {
    } while (*DAT_08000520 != 1);
    *DAT_08000520 = 0;
    *DAT_08000528 = *DAT_08000528 | 1;
    FUN_08001894(DAT_08000524,0);
    FUN_080009f0(10000);
    *DAT_08000528 = *DAT_08000528 & 0xfffffffe;
  } while( true );
}
```

After analyzing the above code, it was reasonable to assume that function FUN_080009f0(10000) was nothing else but the well-known library function HAL_Delay() that takes a single parameter in milliseconds. I assumed that the parameter of this function (=10000) defines the duration of the PWM sequence. Therefore, I assumed that my task could be solved if I changed the parameter from 10000 to 5000. So, I decided to check out this approach.

In order to change the value from 10000 to 50000, I needed to examine the disassembly. As it turned out, the code corresponding to FUN_080009f0() looked like the following (**Fig.22**).

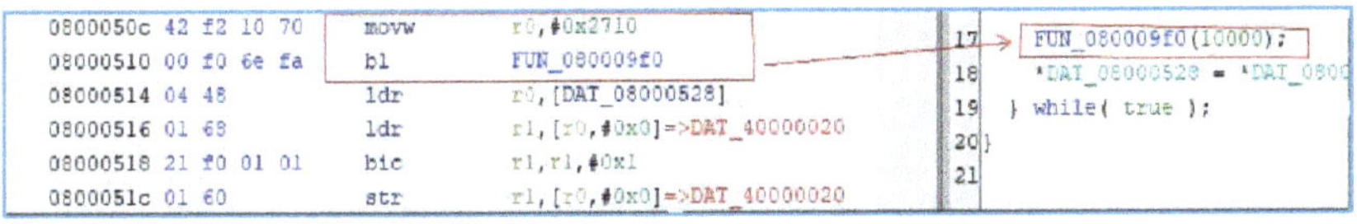

Fig.22

It is seen from that FUN_080009f0() is called using two instructions (**Listing 2**).

Listing 2.

```
0800050c 42 f2 10 70    movw  r0,#0x2710
08000510 00 f0 6e fa    bl    FUN_080009f0
```

To modify the algorithm, I decided to replace the value 0x2710 (=10000) with 0x1388 (=5000) in the **movw** instruction. In order to do that, I right-clicked on this instruction and chose **"Patch Instruction"** (**Fig.23**).

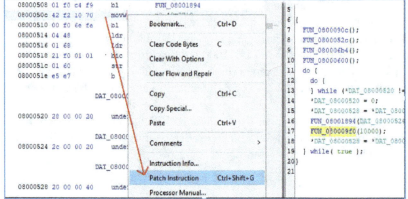

Fig.23

Then in the editor field (**Fig.24**) I replaced 0x2710 with 0x1388.

Fig.24

When I finished editing, the sequence of instructions looked like the following (**Listing 3**).

Listing 3.

```
0800050c 41 f2 88 30    movw    r0,#0x1388
08000510 00 f0 6e fa    bl      FUN_080009f0
```

Then the project was saved, and the modified code was exported into the HEX file **example1patch.hex** by clicking "**Export Program…**" (**Fig.25**).

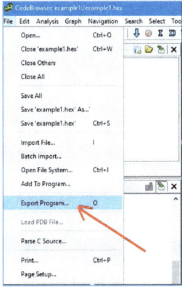

Fig.25

In the opened window I chose **"Intel Hex"** (**Fig.26**).

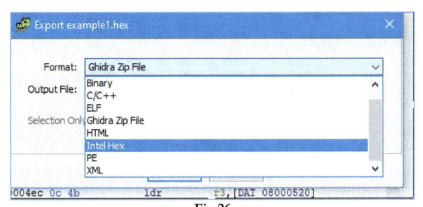

Fig.26

At the next step, the modified code was exported to the file
example1patch.hex (**Fig.27**).

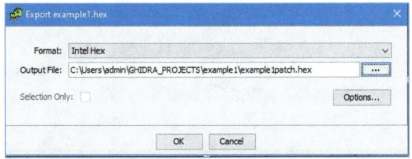

Fig.27

The next window (**Fig.28**) displayed all information concerning the HEX-file.

Fig.28

Then I downloaded the patched HEX-file into the flash memory of the MCU using STM32CubeProgrammer. After the programmer had opened, I chose the **"Open file"** option (**Fig.29**).

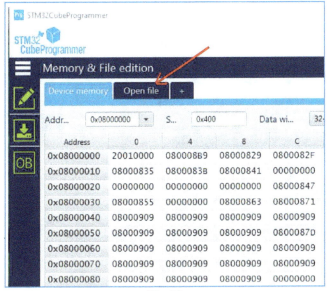

Fig.29

Then, in the dialog box, I chose file **example1patch.hex** (**Fig.30**).

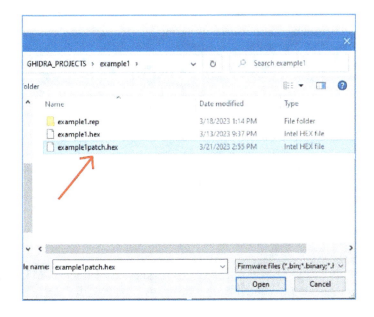

Fig.30

After the contents of the file had been read, I clicked **"Download"** (**Fig.31**).

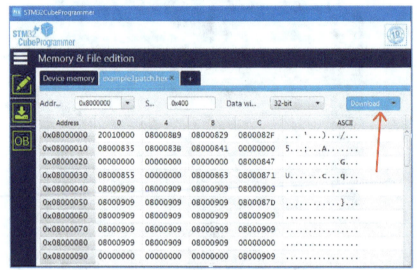

Fig.31

After the operation was completed successfully (**Fig.32**), I reset the board so that I could launch an updated application.

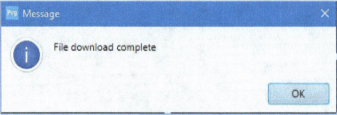

Fig.32

Example 2

The next application board to analyze was equipped with the STM32F722 MCU. One task implemented by this board was to drive the heater as the temperature varied.

The hardware part that was involved included pin **PA0**, where the analog input signal from the temperature sensor arrived. This signal controlled the pulse sequence on pin **PA5** of the microcontroller (**Fig.33**). Pin **PA5**, in turn, drove the oven through a power switch.

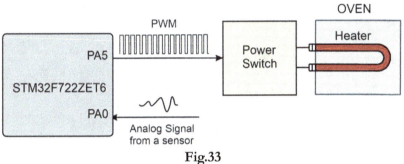

Fig.33

This operation is illustrated in **Fig.34**.

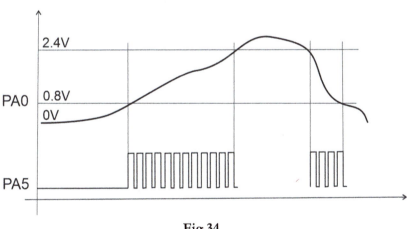

Fig.34

When the voltage level on pin **PA0** had fallen into the range 0.8–2.4 V, the PWM signal on pin **PA5** was enabled. When the input signal on pin **PA0** was less than 0.8 V or greater than 2.4 V, PWM was disabled. Later, the old oven heater was replaced with a new one that should have been driven by PWM when the analog input on pin **PA0** exceeded 0.8 V.

In order to modify the code in the flash memory of the MCU, I used STM32CubeProgrammer and GHIDRA. To save the time that I would spend investigating the board, I also used the Keil uVision Debugger.

Using the uVision Debugger

Using the uVision Debugger helped me quickly examine the peripherals involved in this embedded application. Also, I was going to use the uVision Debugger for testing the application while changing peripheral settings "on the fly".
Therefore, in the Keil uVision IDE I performed the sequence described below.

First, I created a new project as is shown in **Fig.35**.

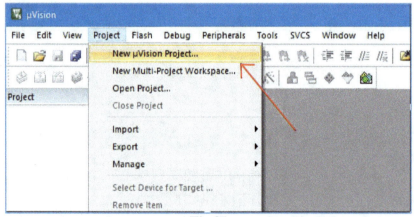

Fig.35

After assigning the name (**example2**) to the project, I chose the target MCU (**Fig.36 - Fig.37**).

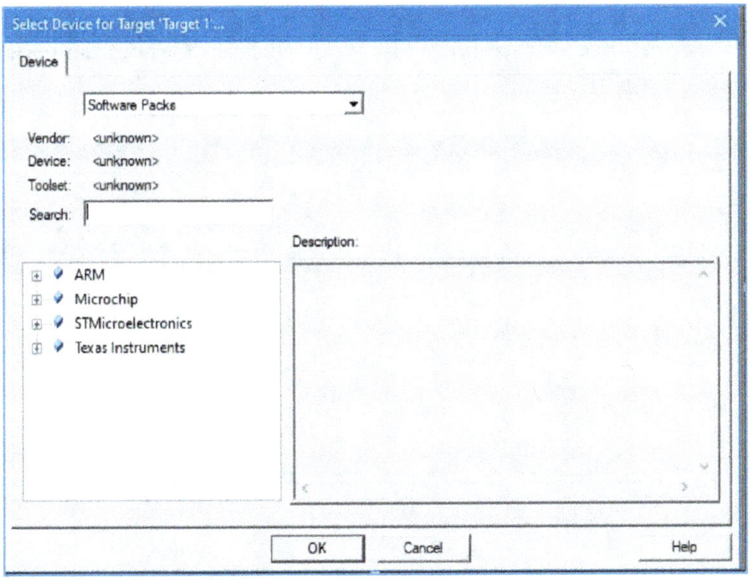

Select Device for Target 'Target 1'...
Device
Software Packs
Vendor: <unknown>
Device: <unknown>
Toolset: <unknown>
Search:
Description:
ARM
Microchip
STMicroelectronics
Texas Instruments
OK
Cancel
Help

Fig.36

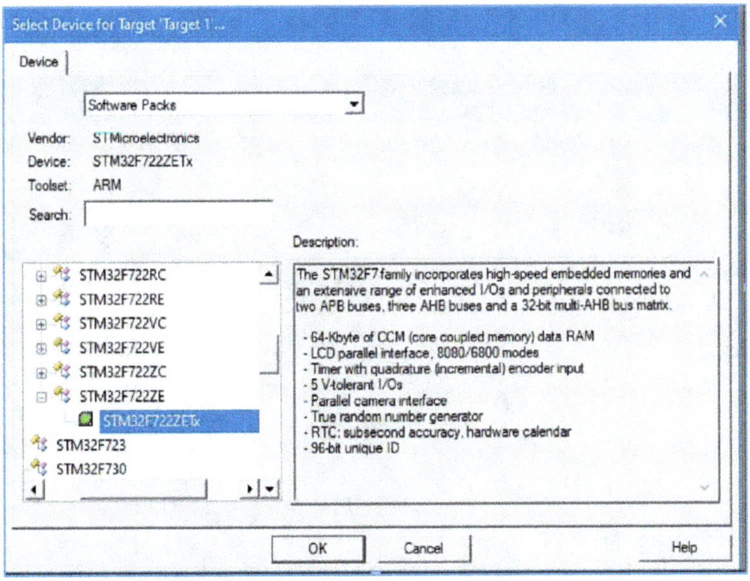

Select Device for Target 'Target 1'...
Device
Software Packs
Vendor: STMicroelectronics
Device: STM32F722ZETx
Toolset: ARM
Search:
Description:
STM32F722RC
STM32F722RE
STM32F722VC
STM32F722VE
STM32F722ZC
STM32F722ZE
STM32F722ZETx
STM32F723
STM32F730
The STM32F7 family incorporates high-speed embedded memories and an extensive range of enhanced I/Os and peripherals connected to two APB buses, three AHB buses and a 32-bit multi-AHB bus matrix.
- 64-Kbyte of CCM (core coupled memory) data RAM
- LCD parallel interface, 8080/6800 modes
- Timer with quadrature (incremental) encoder input
- 5 V-tolerant I/Os
- Parallel camera interface
- True random number generator
- RTC: subsecond accuracy, hardware calendar
- 96-bit unique ID
OK
Cancel
Help

Fig.37

In this particular case, I chose STM32F722ZET6.
Then I skipped the next window (**Fig.38**) by clicking **"Cancel"** and got the empty project (**Fig.39**).

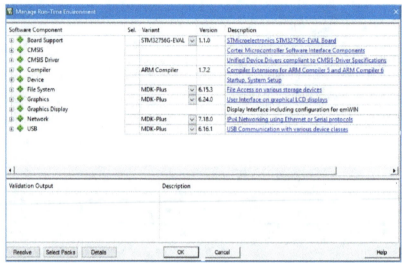

Fig.38

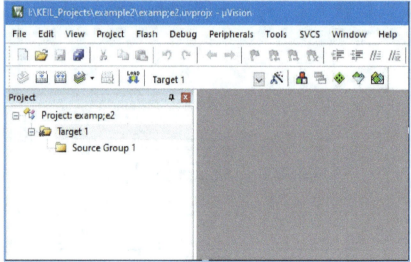

Fig.39

Further, I configured a few options. Since the ST-LINK debug probe was used, I moved to the **"Debug"** page and chose **"ST-Link"** (**Fig.40**).

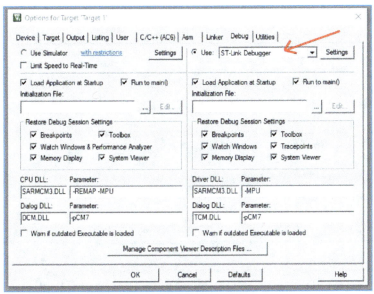

Fig.40

Clicking on **"Settings"** brought me to the **"Driver Setup"** page (**Fig.41**) where I enabled **"Trace Enable"**. The rest of the options were left unchanged.

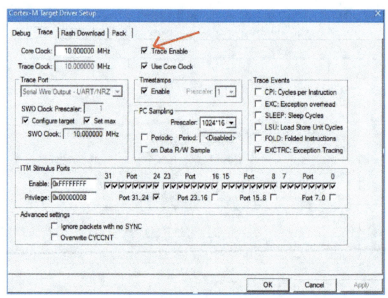

Fig.41

Then, on the "**Debug**" page I disabled two options, "**Load Application at Startup** " and "**Run to main()**" (**Fig.42**). Other options on this page remained the same.

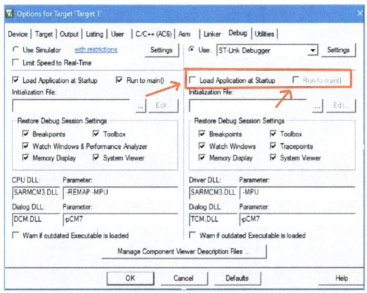

Fig.42

Finally, I disabled the **"Update Target before Debugging"** option (**Fig.43**) on the **"Utilities"** page.

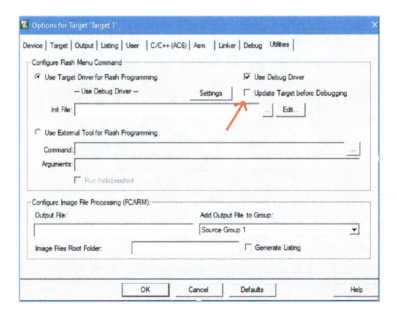

Fig.43

After completing these preliminary steps, I started debugging by clicking on the **"Debug"** icon (**Fig.44**).

Fig.44

To start execution of an application, I clicked the **"Run"** icon (**Fig.45**).

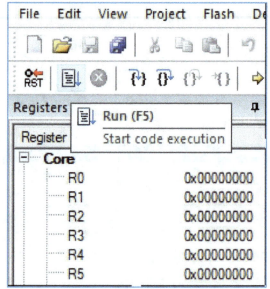

Fig.45

Then I tried to discover how pin **PA5** is driven. It would be reasonable to examine the GPIOA registers ODR and BSRR, therefore I opened the GPIOA Peripherals window (**Fig.46** - **Fig.47**). These registers could contribute to producing the output signal on pin **PA5**.
However, all bits in these registers remained equal to 0 when the signal on pin **PA0** changed between 0-3.3V.

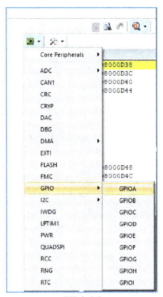

Fig.46

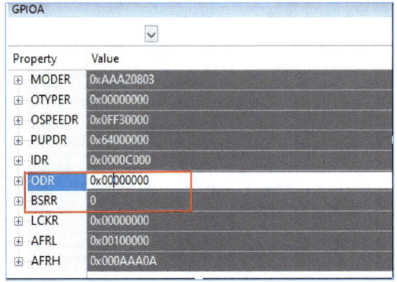

Fig.47

Next, I assumed that pin **PA5** could be controlled by some timer. A few candidates were suggested after looking at the STM32F722ZET microcontroller's datasheet. Then I discovered that Timer 2 **(Fig. 48)** was enabled or disabled when the signal level on input **PA0** changed.

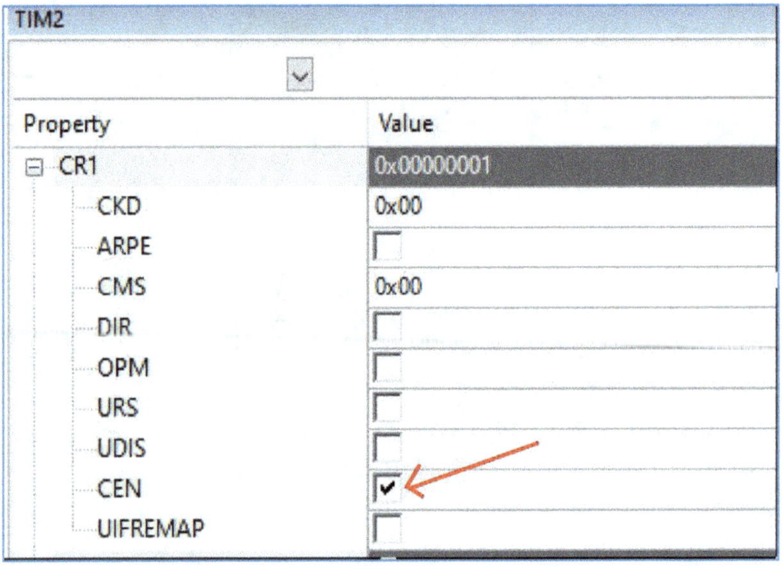

Property	Value
⊟ CR1	0x00000001
CKD	0x00
ARPE	☐
CMS	0x00
DIR	☐
OPM	☐
URS	☐
UDIS	☐
CEN	☑
UIFREMAP	☐

Fig.48

When the input voltage on pin **PA0** was in the range 0.8–2.4 V, bit **CEN** was set (=1), and **PA5** provided the pulse sequence. When the input voltage was out of this range, bit **CEN** was cleared, and **PA5** didn't produce the pulses. Additionally, I examined the CCRx, CCER and CCMRx registers of Timer 2 **(Fig.49)** and concluded that pin **PA5** provided a PWM output signal for Channel 1 of Timer 2.

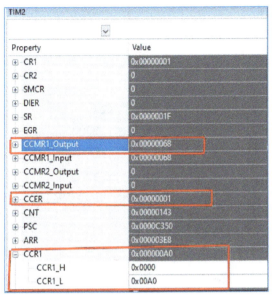

Fig.49

I decided to reverse the embedding code after I had a better understanding of how it worked. Therefore, I used the STM32CubeProgrammer tool to save the code in the HEX-file (called **example2.hex**).

Reversing embedded code

While reversing this file in the GHIDRA Disassembler, I found out the function that resembles **main()** (**Listing 4**).

Listing 4.

```
void FUN_08000524(void)

{
undefined4 uVar1;
FUN_08000d52();
FUN_0800059c();
FUN_080007c4();
FUN_08000678();
```

```
FUN_0800071c();
FUN_08003700();
uVar1 =
FUN_080037d4(PTR_FUN_0800096c+1_0800057c,0,PTR_PTR_s_default
Task_08000578);
*DAT_08000580 = uVar1;
uVar1 =
FUN_080037d4(PTR_FUN_0800097c+1_08000588,0,PTR_PTR_s_myTask
02_08000584);
*DAT_0800058c = uVar1;
uVar1 =
FUN_080037d4(PTR_FUN_080009dc+1_08000594,0,PTR_PTR_s_myTask
03_08000590);
*DAT_08000598 = uVar1;
FUN_08003768();
do {
            /* WARNING: Do nothing block with infinite loop */
} while( true );
}
```

The above code told that this application was designed using RTOS with 3
threads (functions FUN_0800096c, FUN_0800097c, and FUN_080009dc).
Therefore, there is a reason to investigate these functions in more detail; this
could help to find a solution.

Further investigation brought me to the following function (**Listing 5**).

Listing 5.

```
************************************************************
*                      FUNCTION                           *
************************************************************
        undefined FUN_0800097c()
        undefined      r0:1        <RETURN>
        undefined4      Stack[-0xc]:4 local_c  XREF[1]:    08000982(W)
                FUN_0800097c+1     XREF[0,2]
                                   FUN_08000524:08000554(*),
                FUN_0800097c          08000588(*)
0800097c 80 b5      push    {r7,lr}
```

40

```
0800097e 82 b0          sub     sp,#0x8
08000980 00 af          add     r7,sp,#0x0
08000982 78 60          str     r0,[r7,#local_c]
                LAB_08000984        XREF[1]:     080009ce(j)
08000984 12 48          ldr     r0=>DAT_200000c0,[DAT_080009d0]
08000986 00 f0 55 fa    bl      FUN_08000e34  undefined FUN_08000e34()
0800098a 14 21          movs    r1,#0x14
0800098c 10 48          ldr     r0=>DAT_200000c0,[DAT_080009d0]
0800098e 00 f0 1f fb    bl      FUN_08000fd0  undefined FUN_08000fd0()
08000992 0f 48          ldr     r0=>DAT_200000c0,[DAT_080009d0]
08000994 00 f0 a7 fb    bl      FUN_080010e6 undefined FUN_080010e6()
08000998 03 46          mov     r3,r0
0800099a 9a b2          uxth    r2,r3
0800099c 0d 4b          ldr     r3,[DAT_080009d4]
0800099e 1a 80          strh    r2,[r3,#0x0]=>DAT_200000b8
080009a0 0c 4b          ldr     r3,[DAT_080009d4]
080009a2 1b 88          ldrh    r3,[r3,#0x0]=>DAT_200000b8
080009a4 9b b2          uxth    r3,r3
080009a6 b3 f5 7a 7f    cmp.w   r3,#0x3e8
080009aa 0a d9          bls     LAB_080009c2
080009ac 09 4b          ldr     r3,[DAT_080009d4]
080009ae 1b 88          ldrh    r3,[r3,#0x0]=>DAT_200000b8
080009b0 9b b2          uxth    r3,r3
080009b2 40 f6 b7 32    movw    r2,#0xbb7
080009b6 93 42          cmp     r3,r2
080009b8 03 d8          bhi     LAB_080009c2
080009ba 07 4b          ldr     r3=>DAT_200000bc,[DAT_080009d8]
080009bc 01 22          movs    r2,#0x1
080009be 1a 60          str     r2,[r3,#0x0]=>DAT_200000bc
080009c0 02 e0          b       LAB_080009c8
                LAB_080009c2        XREF[2]:     080009aa(j), 080009b8(j)
080009c2 05 4b          ldr     r3=>DAT_200000bc,[DAT_080009d8]
080009c4 00 22          movs    r2,#0x0
080009c6 1a 60          str     r2,[r3,#0x0]=>DAT_200000bc
                LAB_080009c8        XREF[1]:     080009c0(j)
080009c8 14 20          movs    r0,#0x14
080009ca 02 f0 a9 ff    bl      FUN_08003920
undefined FUN_08003920()
080009ce d9 e7          b       LAB_08000984
```

I choose to modify (patch) the instructions in the following disassembly (**Listing 6**).

Listing 6.

```
080009a4 9b b2          uxth     r3,r3
080009a6 b3 f5 7a 7f     cmp.w    r3,#0x3e8
080009aa 0a d9          bls      LAB_080009c2
080009ac 09 4b          ldr      r3,[DAT_080009d4]
080009ae 1b 88          ldrh     r3,[r3,#0x0]=>DAT_200000b8
080009b0 9b b2          uxth     r3,r3
080009b2 40 f6 b7 32     movw     r2,#0xbb7
080009b6 93 42          cmp      r3,r2
080009b8 03 d8          bhi      LAB_080009c2
080009ba 07 4b          ldr      r3=>DAT_200000bc,[DAT_080009d8]
080009bc 01 22          movs     r2,#0x1
080009be 1a 60          str      r2,[r3,#0x0]=>DAT_200000bc
080009c0 02 e0          b        LAB_080009c8
```

To modify the embedded code, I performed the following steps.
1. Inserted the label (called **next**) before instruction

```
080009ba 07 4b          ldr      r3=>DAT_200000bc,[DAT_080009d8]
```

To do that, I right-clicked on this instruction and chose **"Add Label..."** (**Fig.50** - **Fig.51**)).

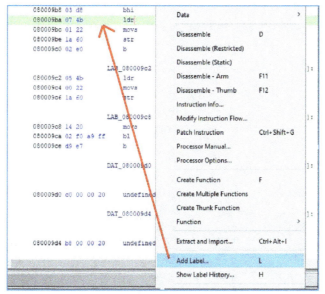

Fig.50

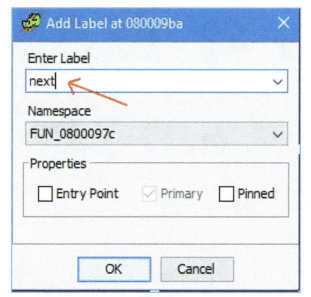

Fig.51

2. Replaced the instruction

080009ac 09 4b   ldr r3,[DAT_080009d4]   = 200000B8h

with

b next

Following that, the disassembly became as follows (**Listing 7**).

Listing 7.

080009a6 b3 f5 7a 7f	cmp.w	r3,#0x3e8	
080009aa 0a d9	bls	LAB_080009c2	
080009ac 05 e0	**b**	**next**	
080009ae 1b 88	ldrh	r3,[r3,#0x0]=>DAT_200000b8	
080009b0 9b b2	uxth	r3,r3	
080009b2 40 f6 b7 32	movw	r2,#0xbb7	
080009b6 93 42	cmp	r3,r2	
080009b8 03 d8	bhi	LAB_080009c2	
	next	XREF[1]: 080009ac(j)	
080009ba 07 4b	ldr	r3=>DAT_200000bc, [DAT_080009d8]	
080009bc 01 22	movs	r2,#0x1	
080009be 1a 60	str	r2,[r3,#0x0]=>DAT_200000bc	
080009c0 02 e0	b	LAB_080009c8	
	LAB_080009c2	XREF[2]: 080009aa(j),	
		080009b8(j)	
080009c2 05 4b	ldr	r3=>DAT_200000bc,[DAT_080009d8]	
080009c4 00 22	movs	r2,#0x0	
080009c6 1a 60	str	r2,[r3,#0x0]=>DAT_200000bc	

After patching the code was complete, I exported the program into the file **example2gh.hex** (**Fig.52** - **Fig.53**).

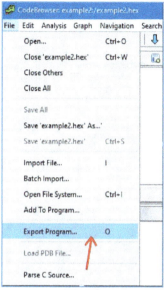

Fig.52

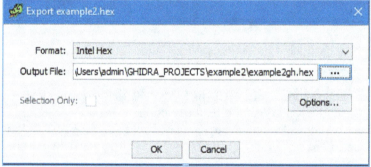

Fig.53

3. Downloaded the file **example2gh.hex** into the MCU's flash memory using the STM32CubeProgrammer tool and restarted the microcontroller.

Example 3

Producing the rectangular sequence on pin **PA5** for approximately 10 seconds was one of the tasks carried out by the next application board with

45

the STM32L476RG microcontroller (**Fig.54** - **Fig.55**). The generation of pulses on pin **PA5** ended after the time interval expired.

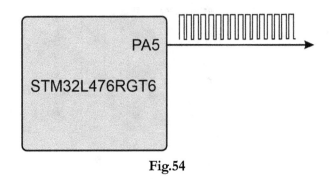

Fig.54

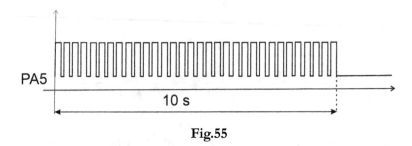

Fig.55

The embedded code of the MCU had to be changed to enable **PA5** forever. Here I used the Keil uVision IDE for analyzing, reverse engineering, patching, and downloading the updated code back into the MCU's flash memory. In order to do that, I used the SEGGER J-Link debug probe.

Using the uVision Debugger

First, I created the new project (called **example3**) in the uVision IDE, then set the options as described in detail in the previous example. The only option that was changed was the type of the debug probe (**Fig.56**).

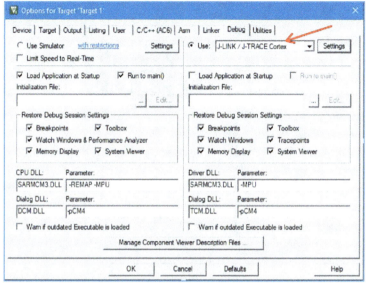

Fig.56

What I was going to do while debugging the code was to find out the
peripherals involved in generating the rectangular pulse sequence on pin
PA5. It seemed logical to assume that some timer could be used to generate
the pulse sequence on this pin.

Analyzing timers while debugging made me sure that pin **PA5** (**Fig.57**)
provided a pulse sequence only when Timer 6 (**Fig.58**) was enabled.

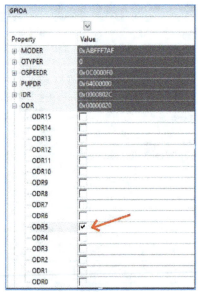

Fig.57

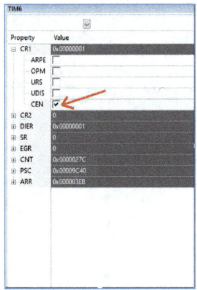

Fig.58

48

It turned out that after 10 s, bit **CEN** was cleared (=0x0), thus stopping Timer 6, and pulse generation on pin **PA5** stopped.

It would be logical to assume that generating the pulse sequence on pin **PA5** would take place after bit **CEN** was set (=0x1). So, I first chose to go through the disassembly to determine the sequence of instructions that disables Timer 6.

While passing through the disassembly, I assumed that the following sequence (**Fig.59**) could affect Timer 6.

```
sassembly                                                            ⚐ ▣
0x080001C2 2000      MOVS      r0,#0x00                                ∧
0x080001C4 2004      MOVS      r0,#0x04
0x080001C6 0800      LSRS      r0,r0,#0
0x080001C8 B580      PUSH      {r7,lr}
0x080001CA AF00      ADD       r7,sp,#0x00
0x080001CC F000F9DA  BL.W      0x08000584
0x080001D0 F000F810  BL.W      0x080001F4
0x080001D4 F000F89A  BL.W      0x0800030C
0x080001D8 F000F85E  BL.W      0x08000298
0x080001DC F2427010  MOVW      r0,#0x2710
0x080001E0 F000FA4C  BL.W      0x0800067C
0x080001E4 4802      LDR       r0,[pc,#8]   ; @0x080001F0
0x080001E6 6801      LDR       r1,[r0,#0x00]
0x080001E8 F0210101  BIC       r1,r1,#0x01
0x080001EC 6001      STR       r1,[r0,#0x00]
0x080001EE E7FE      B         0x080001EE
0x080001F0 1000      ASRS      r0,r0,#0
0x080001F2 4000      ANDS      r0,r0,r0
0x080001F4 B580      PUSH      {r7,lr}
0x080001F6 B096      SUB       sp,sp,#0x58                             ∨
                                                                      >
```

Fig.59

Here, instruction

0x080001E4 4802   LDR   r0,[pc,#8] ; @0x080001F0

loads the data stored at address 0x080001F0 into the core register **r0**. The disassembly gave me a couple of instructions at this address:

0x080001F0 1000   ASRS   r0,r0,#0
0x080001F2 4000   ANDS   r0,r0,r0

These instructions didn't make sense in this case, so I tried to treat them as data. This gave me the value 0x40001000, which was nothing else but the address of the Timer 6 Control Register 1 (TIM6_CR1).

This gave me the value 0x40001000, which was nothing else but the address of the Timer 6 Control Register 1 (TIM6_CR1). In this case, it became clear what the following three instructions did (**Listing 8**).

Listing 8.

```
0x080001E4 4802       LDR     r0,[pc,#8]  ; @0x080001F0
0x080001E6 6801       LDR     r1,[r0,#0x00]
0x080001E8 F0210101 BIC      r1,r1,#0x01
0x080001EC 6001       STR     r1,[r0,#0x00]
```

 The instruction

```
0x080001E6 6801       LDR     r1, [r0,#0x00]
```

loads the data from the TIM6_CR1 register into the core register **r1**. Instruction

```
0x080001E8 F0210101 BIC      r1,r1,#0x01
```

clears bit 0 in register **r1** and instruction

```
0x080001EC 6001       STR     r1,[r0,#0x00]
```

stores the updated data in the TIM6_CR1 register.
This disables Timer 6 because bit 0 (**CEN**) of the TIM6_CR1 register is cleared. It was easy to test this assumption by setting or clearing bit **CEN** and viewing the output pin **PA5** after 10 s expired.
It turned out that setting bit **CEN** after an interval of 10 s enables Timer 6 forever, thus providing pulse generation on pin **PA5**.
At the following step, I tried to replace the instruction

```
0x080001E8 F0210101 BIC      r1,r1,#0x01
```

with a sequence of instructions that didn't change bit 0 in register **r1**.

Since the BIC instruction is represented by 4 bytes (F0210101), only these 4 bytes have to be replaced with the appropriate instruction(s). I used the following instructions:

MOV R1, R1
MOV R1, R1

Each MOV R1, R2 instruction takes 2 bytes (0x0946); therefore the updated fragment would look like the following

0x080001E4 4802	LDR	r0,[pc,#8]	; @0x080001F0
0x080001E6 6801	LDR	r1,[r0,#0x00]	
0x0800001E8 0946	MOV	r1, r1	
0x080001EA 0946	MOV	r1, r1	
0x080001EC 6001	STR	r1,[r0,#0x00]	

Patching embedded code in the uVision Debugger

In order to make these changes in code permanent, I performed the following steps:
1. Opened the **Memory Window (Memory1) (Fig.60)**.

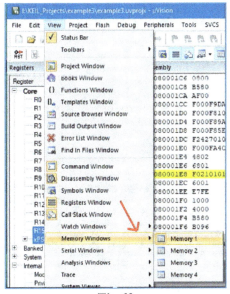

Fig.60

2. In the **Memory1** window, I entered the address **0x80001e8** and got the contents of memory beginning with this address (**Fig.61**).

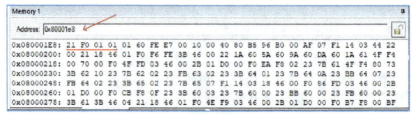

Fig.61

3. In this window, I replaced the sequence of bytes 21F00101 with the sequence 09460946. I made this operation for each of the 4 bytes beginning at the address **0x80001e8**. For example, in order to replace the byte 0x21 at address **0x80001e8** by 0xBF I did the following:
  - Right-clicked on value 0x21 and chose **"Modify Memory at 0x080001E8"** (**Fig.62**).

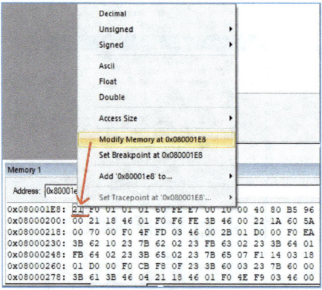

Fig.62

  - In the opened window, I entered 0x09 (**Fig.63**). Next, I repeated the operation by entering 0x46 (**Fig.64**).

52

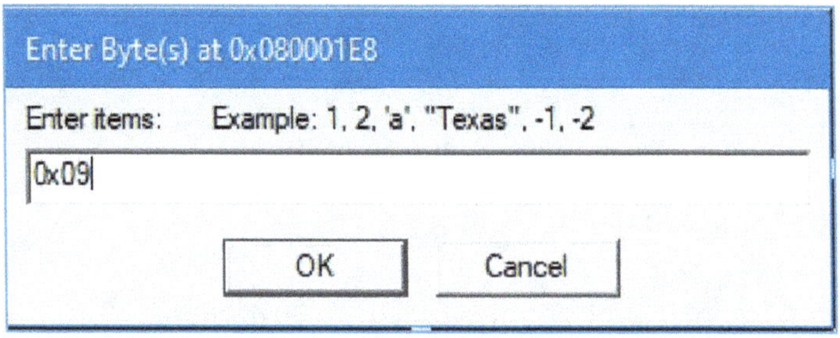

Fig.63

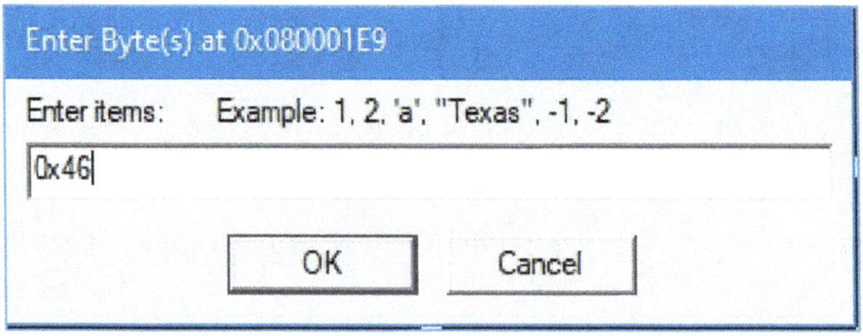

Fig.64

It was easy to check both writing operations in the **Command** window (**Fig.65**).

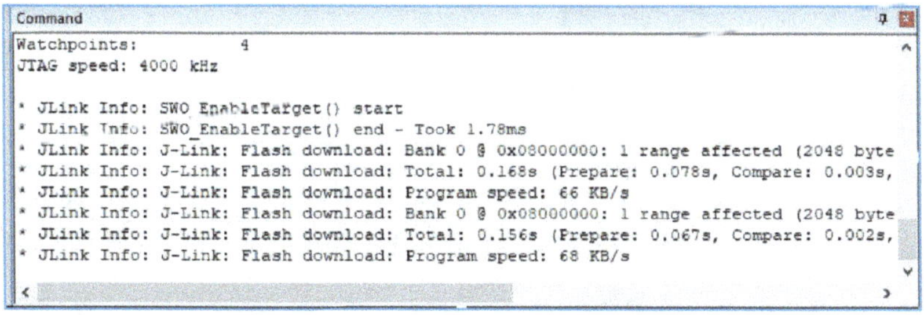

Fig.65

Then I repeated the same operations to write one more instruction MOV to the MCU's flash.

To see how the code altered, I then moved to address **0x080001E4** in the **Disassembly** window (**Fig.66**).

```
0x080001E4 4802      LDR      r0,[pc,#8]   ; @0x080001F0
0x080001E6 6801      LDR      r1,[r0,#0x00]
0x080001E8 4609      MOV      r1,r1
0x080001EA 4609      MOV      r1,r1
0x080001EC 6001      STR      r1,[r0,#0x00]
```

Fig.66

For clarity, I repeated this fragment below:

```
0x080001E4 4802     LDR     r0,[pc,#8]  ; @0x080001F0
0x080001E6 6801     LDR     r1,[r0,#0x00]
0x080001E8 4609     MOV     r1,r1
0x080001EA 4609     MOV     r1,r1
0x080001EC 6001     STR     r1,[r0,#0x00]
```

Finally, I reset the MCU to test the application. The pulse sequence on pin **PA5** never stopped as expected.

There may be one more way to patch the flash memory while debugging. In this case, it is possible to use instruction

B <label>

in order to skip the code fragment that we don't want to be executed.
Let's go back to the following disassembly fragment (**Listing 9**).

Listing 9.

```
0x080001E4 4802        LDR     r0,[pc,#8]  ; @0x080001F0
0x080001E6 6801        LDR     r1,[r0,#0x00]
0x080001E8 F0210101    BIC     r1,r1,#0x01
0x080001EC 6001        STR     r1,[r0,#0x00]
0x080001EE E7FE        B       0x080001EE
```

I already patched the above fragment using two MOV instructions. It is easy to patch the code using only a single branch instruction. This instruction must branch to address 0x080001EE, thus skipping the operation of clearing the **CEN** bit in the TIM6_CR1 register.
The branch instruction could look like the following:

B 0x080001EE

The binary code of this particular instruction is **0xE003**, therefore I should have replaced the binary code **0x4802** of instruction

0x080001E4 4802   LDR   r0,[pc,#8] ; @0x080001F0

with the code **0xE003** that corresponds to instruction

B 0x080001EE

To do that, I moved to the address **0x080001E4** in the **Memory1** window and wrote code **0xE0** at address **0x080001E4** and **0x03** at address 0x080001E5 (**Fig.67** - **Fig.69**).

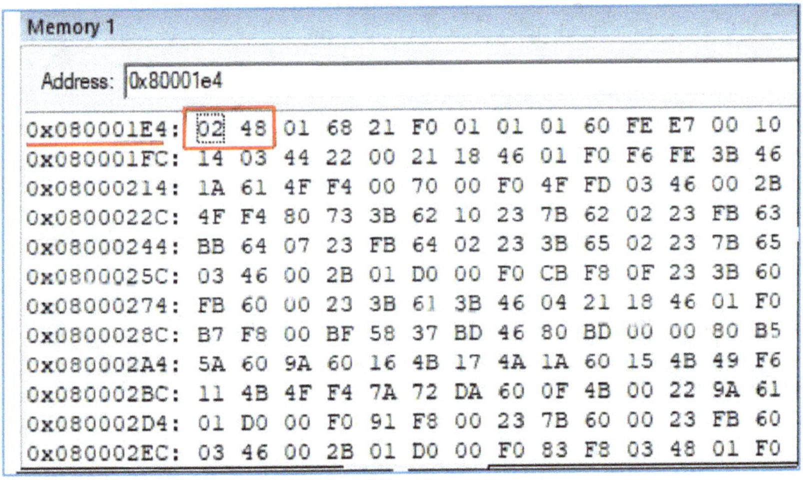

Fig.67

55

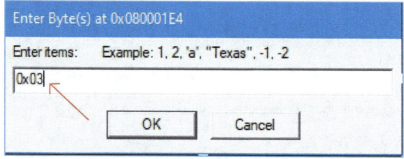

Fig.68

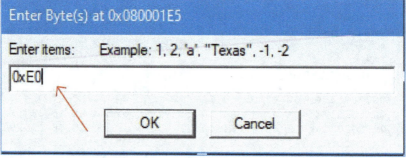

Fig.69

After patching the code was complete, the microcontroller was restarted. When debugging was restarted, the disassembly block looked like the following (**Fig.70**).

```
Disassembly
0x080001D8 F000F85E   BL.W          0x08000298
0x080001DC F2427010   MOVW          r0,#0x2710
0x080001E0 F000FA4C   BL.W          0x0800067C
0x080001E4 E003       B             0x080001EE
0x080001E6 6801       LDR           r1,[r0,#0x00]
0x080001E8 F0210101   BIC           r1,r1,#0x01
0x080001EC 6001       STR           r1,[r0,#0x00]
0x080001EE E7FE       B             0x080001EE
0x080001F0 1000       ASRS          r0,r0,#0
0x080001F2 4000       ANDS          r0,r0,r0
```

Fig.70

For clarity, this fragment is also shown in **Listing 10**.

Listing 10.

```
0x080001E4 E003      B      0x080001EE
0x080001E6 6801      LDR    r1,[r0,#0x00]
0x080001E8 F0210101  BIC    r1,r1,#0x01
0x080001EC 6001      STR    r1,[r0,#0x00]
0x080001EE E7FE      B      0x080001EE
```

It is seen that in the patched code the sequence

```
0x080001E6 6801      LDR    r1,[r0,#0x00]
0x080001E8 F0210101  BIC    r1,r1,#0x01
0x080001EC 6001      STR    r1,[r0,#0x00]
```

will newer be executed. Therefore, the pulse on pin **PA5** will never be stopped.

Example 4

One more power debugging tool that can be used for reverse engineering and debugging microcontrollers is IAR Embedded Workbench IDE. In this example I will show how to apply this tool for analyzing the application board with the STM32F030F4P6 microcontroller.
One of the tasks implemented by this board is to provide the gradual increasing of the pulse width of PWM feeding a light device. This is illustrated in **Fig.71**.

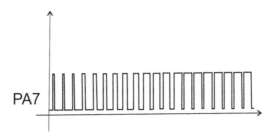

Fig.71

After the microcontroller had been powered on, pin **PA7** provides the PWM signal with the duty cycle that gradually changed approximately from 1% to 97%. When the upper value (97%) reached, the duty cycle of PWM remained the same forever.

I needed to change the embedded code so that the duty cycle stopped to change at value 20% (**Fig.72**).

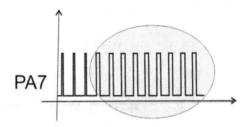

Fig.72

I used IAR Embedded Workbench for ARM (v.9.32) in order to debug, reverse engineering and patch the code. Also, I applied the SEGGER J-Link debug probe.

Before reversing embedded code, I got the HEX-file (called **example4.hex**) using the STM32Cube Programmer tool and ST-LINK debug probe. Then I created a new project in IAR Embedded Workbench IDE as is described further.

Configuring a new project in the IAR Embedded Workbench IDE

First, I created a new project in IAR Embedded Workbench IDE by clicking (**Fig.73**).

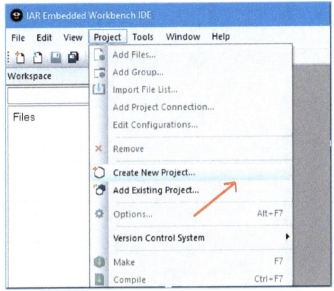

Fig.73

Then I chose the **"Externally built executable"** project template (**Fig.74**).

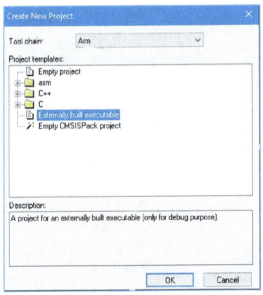

Fig.74

At the next step, I chose the folder where to place the project files and assigned the example4 name to the project (**Fig.75**).

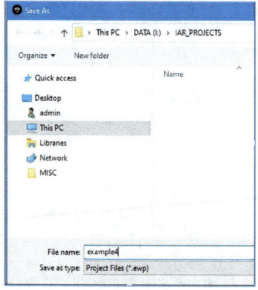

Fig.75

Finally, I obtained the empty project (**Fig.76**).

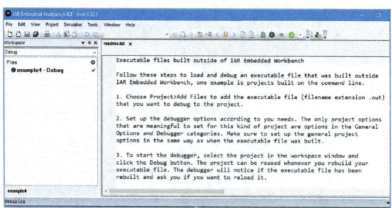

Fig.76

Then I needed to configure a few options (**Fig.77**).

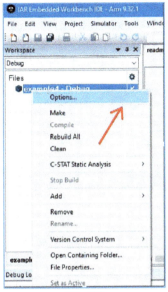

Fig.77

In the next windows (**Fig.78** - **Fig.80**), I chose the type of the microcontroller (STM32F030F4).

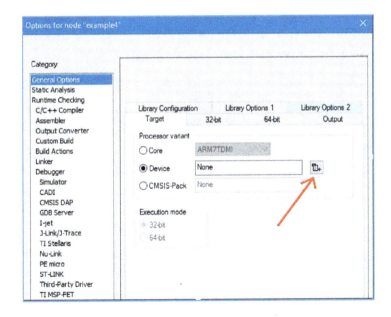

Fig.78

Mediatek	ST STM32F030C6	STM32F0x0	>
Microchip	ST STM32F030C8	STM32F0x1	>
Micronas	ST STM32F030CC	STM32F0x2	>
Microsemi	ST STM32F030F4	STM32F0x8	>
MindMotion	ST STM32F030K6	STSPIN32F0	>

Fig.79

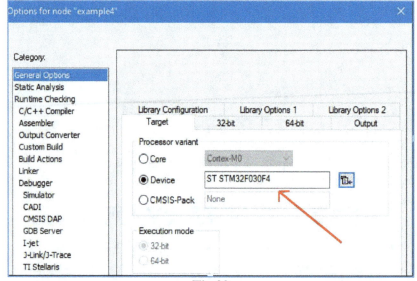

Fig.80

Since I was going to apply the DEGGER J-Link debug probe , I chose "J-Link" as a debugger (**Fig.81**).

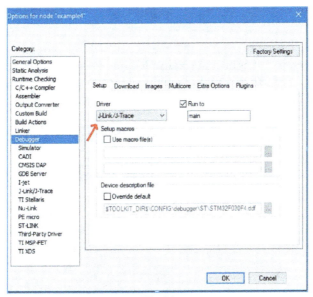

Fig.81

I also opened the additional window (**Fig.82**) that gave me the additional options for J-Link, but I decided to leave them unchanged.

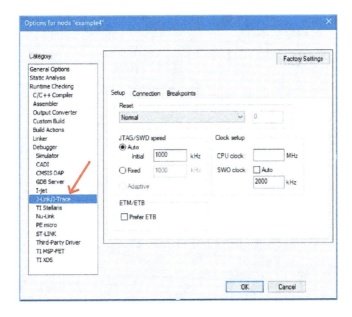

Fig.82

This type of a project requires that the binary file should be added to the project. Therefore, I copied the **example4.hex** file obtained from STM32CubeProgrammer tool to the folder where the project files were placated. Then I added this file to the project (**Fig.83 - Fig.84**).

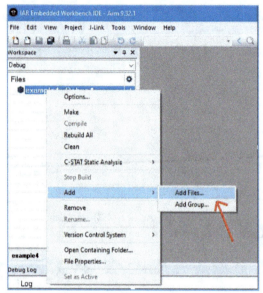

Fig.83

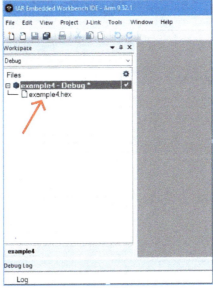

Fig.84

At this point, it became possible to begin reversing embedded code.

Patching embedded code in the IAR Embedded Workbench IDE

Next, I began debugging by choosing **"Debug without Downloading"** to examine peripherals and embedded code (**Fig.85**).

Fig.85

When debugging began, I received the following message (**Fig.86**).

Fig.86

Also, in the **Debugger Log** window I got one more warning "Could not go to main" (**Fig.87**).

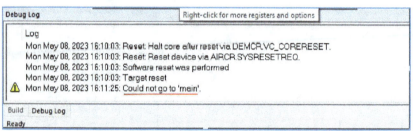

Fig.87

This meant that I could meet the challenges while analyzing embedded code. First what I wanted to do was to find out the peripherals that control pin **PA7**. I assumed that the PWM signal on pin **PA7** could be generated by some timer; therefore, I went through timers using the **Register1** window (**Fig.88**).

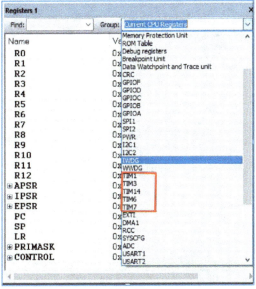

Fig.88

Then I found out that the pulse width on Channel 2 of Timer 3 (register TIM3_CCR2, **Fig.89**) gradually changed and became stable at value 0x1 (=97). Also, I discovered that pin **PA7** belonged to Channel 1, so I decided to further investigate the code affecting Timer 3.

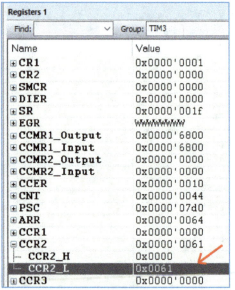

Fig.89

Eventually, I found the disassembly block that could affect the pulse width (**Fig.90**).

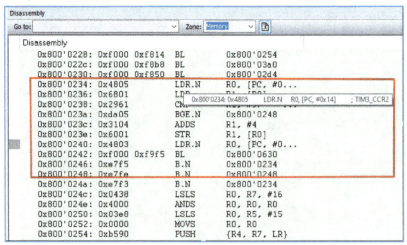

Fig.90

For convenience, this disassembly block is shown in **Listing 11**.

Listing 11.

```
0x800'0234: 0x4805        LDR.N    R0, [PC, #0x14]    ; TIM3_CCR2
0x800'0236: 0x6801        LDR      R1, [R0]
0x800'0238: 0x2961        CMP      R1, #97          ; 0x61
0x800'023a: 0xda05        BGE.N    0x800'0248
0x800'023c: 0x3104        ADDS     R1, #4
0x800'023e: 0x6001        STR      R1, [R0]
0x800'0240: 0x4803        LDR.N    R0, [PC, #0xc]    ; 0x3e8 (1000)
0x800'0242: 0xf000 0xf9f5 BL       0x800'0630
0x800'0246: 0xe7f5        B.N      0x800'0234
0x800'0248: 0xe7fe        B.N      0x800'0248
0x800'024a: 0xe7f3        B.N      0x800'0234
```

After analyzing the above disassembly, I concluded that I could solve the problem by modifying the instruction

```
0x800'0238: 0x2961        CMP      R1, #97          ; 0x61
```

I decided to replace the value 97(=0x61) in this instruction with the value 20 (-0x14). In this case, the CMP instruction would look like the following

```
0x800'0238: 0x2920        CMP      R1, #20
```

To do that, I needed to change only a single byte in instruction CMP. At the next step, I opened the **Memory1** window (**Fig.91**) and moved to address 0x08000238 where the code (-0x2962) of instruction CMP was stored (**Fig.92**).

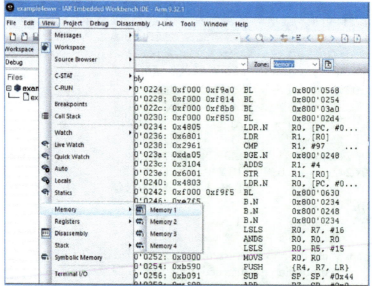

Fig.91

Memory 1

| Go to | 0x08000238 | | Memory | | | |

```
0x0800'0230  00 f0 50 f8 05 48 01 68 61 29 05 da 04 31 01 60
0x0800'0240  03 48 00 f0 f5 f9 f5 e7 fe e7 f3 e7 38 04 00 40
0x0800'0250  e8 03 00 00 90 b5 91 b0 00 af 10 24 3b 19 18 00
0x0800'0260  30 23 1a 00 00 21 01 f0 0b fd 3b 00 18 00 10 23
0x0800'0270  1a 00 00 21 01 f0 04 fd 21 00 7b 18 02 22 1a 60
0x0800'0280  7b 18 01 22 da 60 7b 18 10 22 1a 61 7b 18 00 22
0x0800'0290  1a 62 7b 18 18 00 00 f0 13 fc 03 1e 01 d0 00 f0
```

Fig.92

Byte 0x61 (=97) in the CMP instruction specifies the value to be compared with the contents of register R1. I simply replaced this byte as illustrated in **Fig.93 - Fig.94**.

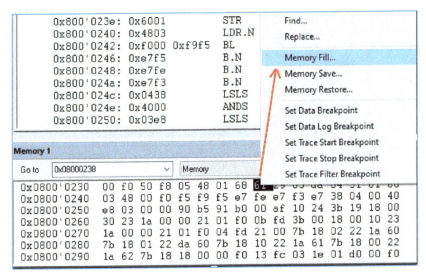

Fig.93

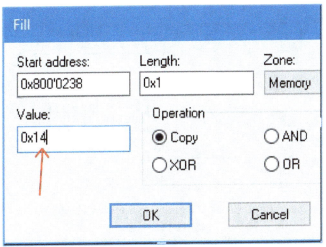

Fig.94

To check the updates, I restarted the debug session and went to address 0x08000238 to verify that the patched code for the instruction CMP was saved in the MCU's flash memory (**Fig. 95**).

```
0x800'0234:  0x4805          LDR.N    R0, [PC, #0...
0x800'0236:  0x6801          LDR      R1, [R0]
0x800'0238:  0x2914          CMP      R1, #20      ...
0x800'023a:  0xda05          BGE.N    0x800'0248
0x800'023c:  0x3104          ADDS     R1, #4
0x800'023e:  0x6001          STR      R1, [R0]
0x800'0240:  0x4803          LDR.N    R0, [PC, #0...
0x800'0242:  0xf000 0xf9f5   BL       0x800'0630
0x800'0246:  0xe7f5          B.N      0x800'0234
0x800'0248:  0xe7fe          B.N      0x800'0248
```

Fig.95

Example 5

The STM32G030F6P6 microcontroller-equipped application board carried out the task represented by the following diagram (**Fig. 96**).

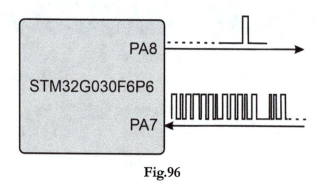

Fig.96

The timing diagram of the I/O signals is shown in **Fig.97**.

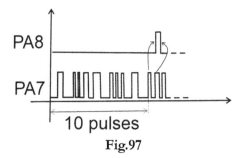

Fig.97

The application counted the pulses arriving on pin **PA7**. If the number of pulses exceeded 10, the **PA8** pin went high.

Pin **PA8** kept high until the next rising edge arrived on pin **PA7**. Then **PA8** went low and stayed in this state until the next 10 pulses were counted.

After the device controlled by pin **PA8** was replaced with the new one, it became necessary to reverse the pulse on this pin, as shown in **Fig.98**.

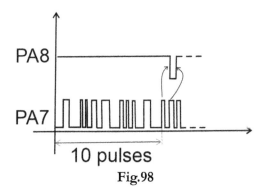

Fig.98

My task was to modify the embedded code so that pin **PA8** would produce the inversed pulse. To modify the embedded code, I used IAR Embedded Workbench. I got the HEX-file (**example5.hex**) using the STM32CubeProgrammer tool and created the project called example5 in the IAR Embedded Workbench IDE.

Analyzing embedded code in the IAR Embedded Workbench IDE

After adding the **example5.hex** file to the project, I started debugging the code by clicking **"Debug without Downloading"** (**Fig.99**).

Fig.99

In this project, I utilized the capabilities of the SEGGER J-Link debug probe to achieve the best results. While debugging, I intended to find the disassembly block that toggled pin **PA8**. While analyzing peripherals, I got a clue after viewing the EXTI rising trigger selection register (EXTI_RTSR1, **Fig. 100**).

Name	Value	Access
RTSR1	0x0000'0080	ReadWrite
RT16	0	ReadWrite
RT15		adWrite
RT14		adWrite
RT13		adWrite
RT12		adWrite
RT11		adWrite
RT10		adWrite
RT9		adWrite
RT8	0	ReadWrite
RT7	1	ReadWrite
RT6	0	ReadWrite
RT5	0	ReadWrite
RT4	0	ReadWrite
RT3	0	ReadWrite
RT2	0	ReadWrite
RT1	0	ReadWrite
RT0	0	ReadWrite

RTSR1.RT16 / RT16
ReadWrite @ 0x4002'1800
bit [16]
Rising trigger event configuration bit of Configurable Event input

Right-click for more registers and options

Fig.100

It turned out that bit 7 (RT7) of this register was set, thus enabling the rising edge trigger for the event and interrupt on the corresponding line. Then I tested how the output signal on pin **PA8** changed when bit RT7 was set / cleared (**Fig.101** - **Fig.102**).

RT8	0	ReadWrite
RT7	1	ReadWrite
RT6	0	ReadWrite

Fig.101

RT8	0	ReadWrite
RT7	0	ReadWrite
RT6	0	ReadWrite

Fig.102

When bit RT7 was set and the pulse train arrived on pin **PA7**, **PA8** toggled as expected. When RT7 was cleared, no changes on pin **PA8** were observed, even when pulses kept going to pin **PA7**.

I assumed that each pulse arriving on pin **PA7** triggered an interrupt, so I decided to search for the code belonging to the Interrupt Service Handler (ISR) that processed the interrupt on this pin.

Finally, I found the disassembly block that could be associated with ISR (**Listing 12**).

Listing 12.

```
0x800'057c: 0xb580        PUSH    {R7, LR}
0x800'057e: 0xaf00        ADD     R7, SP, #0x0
0x800'0580: 0x2080        MOVS    R0, #128        ; 0x80
0x800'0582: 0xf000 0xfb49 BL      0x800'0c18
0x800'0586: 0xb407        PUSH    {R0-R2}
0x800'0588: 0x4810        LDR.N   R0, [PC, #0x40]   ; 0x5000'0014
0x800'058a: 0x6801        LDR     R1, [R0]
0x800'058c: 0x4a10        LDR.N   R2, [PC, #0x40]   ; 0x100 (256)
0x800'058e: 0x4011        ANDS    R1, R1, R2
0x800'0590: 0x2900        CMP     R1, #0
0x800'0592: 0xd100        BNE.N   0x800'0596
0x800'0594: 0xe000        B.N     0x800'0598
0x800'0596: 0x4391        BICS    R1, R1, R2
0x800'0598: 0x6001        STR     R1, [R0]
0x800'059a: 0xbc07        POP     {R0-R2}
```

```
0x800'059c: 0x4b0a    LDR.N    R3, [PC, #0x28]    ; 0x2000'0074
0x800'059e: 0x681b    LDR      R3, [R3]
0x800'05a0: 0x1c5a    ADDS     R2, R3, #1
0x800'05a2: 0x4b09    LDR.N    R3, [PC, #0x24]    ; 0x2000'0074
0x800'05a4: 0x601a    STR      R2, [R3]
0x800'05a6: 0x4b08    LDR.N    R3, [PC, #0x20]    ; 0x2000'0074
0x800'05a8: 0x681b    LDR      R3, [R3]
0x800'05aa: 0x2b0a    CMP      R3, #10            ; 0xa
0x800'05ac: 0xd909    BLS.N    0x800'05c2
0x800'05ae: 0x4b06    LDR.N    R3, [PC, #0x18]    ; 0x2000'0074
0x800'05b0: 0x2200    MOVS     R2, #0
0x800'05b2: 0x601a    STR      R2, [R3]
0x800'05b4: 0xb407    PUSH     {R0-R2}
0x800'05b6: 0x4805    LDR.N    R0, [PC, #0x14]    ; 0x5000'0014
0x800'05b8: 0x6801    LDR      R1, [R0]
0x800'05ba: 0x4a05    LDR.N    R2, [PC, #0x14]    ; 0x100 (256)
0x800'05bc: 0x4311    ORRS     R1, R1, R2
0x800'05be: 0x6001    STR      R1, [R0]
0x800'05c0: 0xbc07    POP      {R0-R2}
0x800'05c2: 0x46c0    MOV      R8, R8
0x800'05c4: 0x46bd    MOV      SP, R7
0x800'05c6: 0xbd80    POP      {R7, PC}
```

Patching embedded code in the IAR Embedded Workbench IDE

After looking over the disassembly shown above, three instructions caught my eye:

```
0x800'0592: 0xd100    BNE.N    0x800'0596

0x800'0596: 0x4391    BICS     R1, R1, R2

0x800'05aa: 0x2b0a    CMP      R3, #10

0x800'05bc: 0x4311    ORRS     R1, R1, R2
```

I thought that it would take three steps to reverse the polarity of the output signal on pin **PA8**. The steps are described in the following order:

1. replacing the BNE.N instruction located at address 0x0800'0592 with BEQ.
2. replacing the BICS instruction located at address 0x0800'0596 with ORRS.
3. replacing the ORRS instruction located at address 0x800'05bc with BICS.

To replace BNE.N with BEQ, I opened the **Memory1** window (**Fig.103**), then moved to address 0x8000593 and replaced byte 0xd1 with 0xd0 (**Fig.104**).

```
Memory 1                                                            ✕

Go to  0x8000596              ∨    Memory          ∨   ▼  ⬆  ➡

0x0800'0560   80 bd 80 b5 00 af c0 46    .......F     ^
0x0800'0568   bd 46 80 bd 80 b5 00 af    .F......
0x0800'0570   00 f0 d6 f8 c0 46 bd 46    .....F.F
0x0800'0578   80 bd 00 00 80 b5 00 af    ........
0x0800'0580   80 20 00 f0 49 fb 07 b4    . ..I...
0x0800'0588   10 48 01 68 10 4a 11 40    .H.h.J.@
0x0800'0590   00 29 00 d1 00 e0 11 43    .).[].. .C
0x0800'0598   01 60 07 bc 0a 4b 1b 68    .`...K.h
0x0800'05a0   5a 1c 09 4b 1a 60 08 4b    Z..K.`.K
0x0800'05a8   1b 68 0a 2b 09 d9 06 4b    .h.+...K
0x0800'05b0   00 22 1a 60 07 b4 05 48    ."..`...H
0x0800'05b8   01 68 05 4a 91 43 01 60    .h.J.C.`
0x0800'05c0   07 bc c0 46 bd 46 80 bd    ...F.F..
0x0800'05c8   74 00 00 20 14 00 00 50    t.. ...P
0x0800'05d0   00 01 00 00 80 b5 00 af    ........
0x0800'05d8   03 4b 18 00 01 f0 64 f9    .K....d.     ∨
```

Fig.103

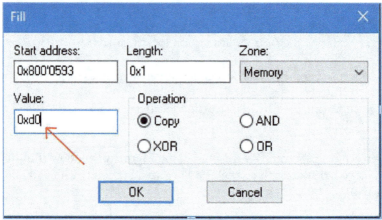

Fig.104

To replace BICS with ORRS, I moved to address 0x08000596 in the **Memory1** window (**Fig.105**) and replaced byte 0x91 with 0x11 (**Fig.106**).

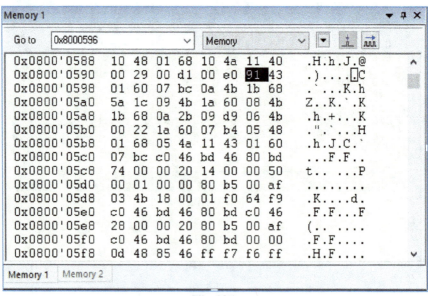

Fig.105

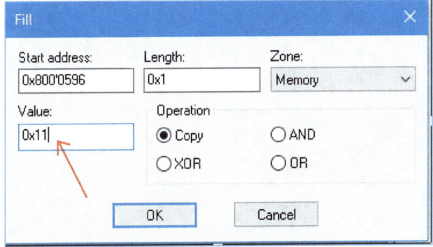

Fig.106

To replace ORRS with BICS, I moved to address 0x80005bc (**Fig.107**) and replaced byte 0x11 with 0x91 (**Fig.108**).

```
Memory 1                                          ▼ ⊥ ×
Go to   0x8000596          ∨   Memory        ∨  ▼  ⊥ ⇥
0x0800'0588   10 48 01 68 10 4a 11 40   .H.h.J.@    ^
0x0800'0590   00 29 00 d1 00 e0 11 43   .).....C
0x0800'0598   01 60 07 bc 0a 4b 1b 60   .`...K.h
0x0800'05a0   5a 1c 09 4b 1a 60 08 4b   Z..K.`.K
0x0800'05a8   1b 68 0a 2b 09 d9 06 4b   .h.+...K
0x0800'05b0   00 22 1a 60 07 b4 05 48   ."..`...H
0x0800'05b8   01 68 05 4a ▉▉ 43 01 60   .h.J.C.`
0x0800'05c0   07 bc c0 46 bd 46 80 bd   ...F.F..
0x0800'05c8   74 00 00 20 14 00 00 50   t.. ...P
0x0800'05d0   00 01 00 00 80 b5 00 af   ........
0x0800'05d8   03 4b 18 00 01 f0 64 f9   .K....d.
0x0800'05e0   c0 46 bd 46 80 bd c0 46   .F.F...F
0x0800'05e8   28 00 00 20 80 b5 00 af   (.. ....
0x0800'05f0   c0 46 bd 46 80 bd 00 00   .F.F....
0x0800'05f8   0d 48 85 46 ff f7 f6 ff   .H.F....    ∨
Memory 1   Memory 2
```

Fig.107

79

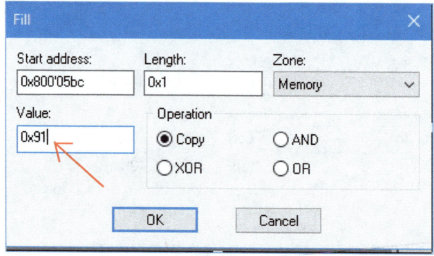

Fig.108

After I had patched these instructions, I started debugging again to ensure that the updated code worked as expected.

The disassembly block with the updated instructions changed to the following (**Listing 13**).

Listing 13.

```
0x800'057c: 0xb580       PUSH    {R7, LR}
0x800'057e: 0xaf00       ADD     R7, SP, #0x0
0x800'0580: 0x2080       MOVS    R0, #128        ; 0x80
0x800'0582: 0xf000 0xfb49 BL      0x800'0c18
0x800'0586: 0xb407       PUSH    {R0-R2}
0x800'0588: 0x4810       LDR.N   R0, [PC, #0x40]    ; 0x5000'0014
0x800'058a: 0x6801       LDR     R1, [R0]
0x800'058c: 0x4a10       LDR.N   R2, [PC, #0x40]    ; 0x100 (256)
0x800'058e: 0x4011       ANDS    R1, R1, R2
0x800'0590: 0x2900       CMP     R1, #0
0x800'0592: 0xd000       BEQ.N   0x800'0596
0x800'0594: 0xe000       B.N     0x800'0598
0x800'0596: 0x4311       ORRS    R1, R1, R2
0x800'0598: 0x6001       STR     R1, [R0]
0x800'059a: 0xbc07       POP     {R0-R2}
0x800'059c: 0x4b0a       LDR.N   R3, [PC, #0x28]    ; 0x2000'0074
```

```
0x800'059e: 0x681b      LDR      R3, [R3]
0x800'05a0: 0x1c5a      ADDS     R2, R3, #1
0x800'05a2: 0x4b09      LDR. N   R3, [PC, #0x24]    ; 0x2000'0074
0x800'05a4: 0x601a      STR      R2, [R3]
0x800'05a6: 0x4b08      LDR.N    R3, [PC, #0x20]    ; 0x2000'0074
0x800'05a8: 0x681b      LDR      R3, [R3]
0x800'05aa: 0x2b0a      CMP      R3, #10            ; 0xa
0x800'05ac: 0xd909      BLS.N    0x800'05c2
0x800'05ae: 0x4b06      LDR.N    R3, [PC, #0x18]    ; 0x2000'0074
0x800'05b0: 0x2200      MOVS     R2, #0
0x800'05b2: 0x601a      STR      R2, [R3]
0x800'05b4: 0xb407      PUSH     {R0-R2}
0x800'05b6: 0x4805      LDR.N    R0, [PC, #0x14]    ; 0x5000'0014
0x800'05b8: 0x6801      LDR      R1, [R0]
0x800'05ba: 0x4a05      LDR.N    R2, [PC, #0x14]    ; 0x100 (256)
0x800'05bc: 0x4391      BICS     R1, R1, R2
0x800'05be: 0x6001      STR      R1, [R0]
0x800'05c0: 0xbc07      POP      {R0-R2}
0x800'05c2: 0x46c0      MOV      R8, R8
0x800'05c4: 0x46bd      MOV      SP, R7
0x800'05c6: 0xbd80      POP      {R7, PC}
```

In the above disassembly, the patched instructions were as follows:

```
0x800'0592: 0xd000      BEQ.N    0x800'0596

0x800'0596: 0x4311      ORRS     R1, R1, R2

0x800'05bc: 0x4391      BICS     R1, R1, R2
```

Index

www.ingramcontent.com/pod-product-compliance
Lightning Source LLC
LaVergne TN
LVHW051644050326
832903LV00022B/876